THE CONNECTION

THI

EVERGREEN BOOKS LT.

LONDO.

Introduction by
Kenneth Tynan

Photographs by
John E. Wulp

CONNECTION

A PLAY BY JACK GELBER

GROVE PRESS, INC.
NEW YORK

Copyright © 1957 by Jack Gelber
Introduction © 1960 by Kenneth Tynan

CAUTION: This play is fully protected, in whole, in part or in
 any form under the copyright laws of the United States
 of America, The British Empire including the Dominion
 of Canada, and all other countries of the Copyright
 Union, and is subject to royalty. All rights, including
 professional, amateur, motion picture, radio, television,
 recitation, public reading are strictly reserved. All in-
 quiries should be addressed to the author's represent-
 ative:
 Seymour Litvinoff, Esq., 10 East 53 Street, New York 22,
 N. Y.

Library of Congress Catalog Card Number: 60-8711

First Evergreen Edition 1960

Twelfth Printing

MANUFACTURED IN THE UNITED STATES OF AMERICA

DISTRIBUTED BY RANDOM HOUSE, INC., NEW YORK

CAROLE

PREFACE

In Moscow — or so they told me when I was there five years ago — you do not say to a friend: "Let's go to the Art Theatre and see 'The Three Sisters.'" Instead, you say: "Let's drop in at the Art Theatre and see how those sisters are getting on." I realized why as soon as I saw the celebrated Nemirovich-Danchenko production of Chekhov's play. The stage exuded a sense of life, pre-existent and continuing; it was not like going to the theatre, it was like paying a call on old acquaintances. I seemed to have met these people long before the curtain rose, and after it fell I found myself wondering what would become of them. I feel much the same, *mutatis mutandis*, about "The Connection."

I first saw Jack Gelber's play in August, 1959. It had opened at the Living Theatre on Sixth Avenue about five weeks earlier, when it had received a fairly thorough bludgeoning from the daily press. A small cult of devotees, however, had formed around it, and it was on the recommendation of one of them that I went. Since then the cult has snowballed. As I write, six months later, it has developed into an obsession for some of its members, and there are few prominent Broadway figures who would admit, with anything like pride, that they had not seen the play. It has pervaded the consciousness of many people who had hitherto thought themselves immune to experimental theatre. It has become, in short, a cultural must. A few weekly reviewers gave it lavish praise; otherwise, it has had to depend for its success entirely on its own merits, supported by that most potent and unpredictable of critics, word of mouth.

"The Connection" is a difficult play to write about. Its atmosphere somewhat recalls Gorky's "Lower Depths"; its theme is akin to that of "Waiting for Godot"; and it tackles the same social problem as "A Hatful of Rain." But to say what a work of art is *like* is often a tacit confession of inability to say what it *is*. Starkly yet unsensationally, compassionately yet unsentimentally, Mr. Gelber's play deals with a subject that the theatre (or the cinema, or television) hardly ever approaches except as a pretext for pathetic melodrama. The people with whom it is concerned are beyond the reach of drama, as we commonly define the word. They are heroin addicts, from which it follows that they are almost totally passive as human beings; their lives are spent in expectation of the next "fix," the next moment of glorious, transient reconciliation with the world and with themselves. They see themselves neither as victims nor as heroes, but merely as absentees from the daytime universe; their relationship to society is not one of enmity, but one of truancy. While they wait for their dope-purveyor — or "connection" — to arrive, they idly debate their condition. "That taste," one of them muses, "that little taste. If you don't find it there you look some place else. And you're running, man. Running . . . I used to think that the people who walk the streets, the people who work every day, the people who worry so much about the next dollar, the next new coat, the next vitamin, the chlorophyll addicts, the aspirin addicts, those people are hooked worse than me . . ." "They are," says a fellow junkie. "Man, they sure are. You happen to have a vice that is illegal." Later, the long-awaited connection turns up, and offers a sour comment on the official attitude toward narcotics: "Everything that's illegal is illegal because it makes more money for more people that way."

The play is not a defence of dope. Nor does it attack the wage-earning, clock-punching, home-making technique of survival; as one of the characters says, " . . . what's wrong with day jobs? Or being square? Man, I haven't anything against them. There are lousy hipsters and lousy squares." Leach, the snarling, snickering, putatively epicene hipster in whose apartment the play unfolds, has built up such a tolerance to drugs that he can no longer get high; and one of the most shattering moments of the stage production is that in which, tightening a belt around his arm to bring up the necessary vein, he gives himself an overdose that very nearly kills him. There is no softening of the agony. But equally, there is no shirking of the issues. The junkie seeks euphoria. The average citizen seeks happiness. How do these goals essentially differ? If the aim of life is pleasure, why is it more desirable to achieve it by injecting dollars into the bank account than by injecting dope into the bloodstream? If, on the other hand, the aim is spiritual enlightenment, how can we be sure that the insights provided by heroin (or mescalin, so eloquently hymned by Aldous Huxley) are less reliable than those supplied by religious mysticism? "The Connection" offers no answers; it simply states the problem, and implies the questions.

Theatrical characters — even inactive ones — must talk;

and junkies, as a class, are contemplative rather than talk-ative. To overcome this handicap, Mr. Gelber employs the device of a play within a play. A nervous producer explains to us that he has hired a writer to bring together a group of addicts for the express purpose of improvising dialogue along lines that the author has previously laid down. The results are filmed, before our eyes, by a two-man camera crew. There are thus, acting as a collective bridge between us and the junkies, four intruders from the world of getting and spending. Some of them, by the end of the evening, have surrendered their credentials as squares and allowed themselves to be drawn into the hipsters' orbit. In the interim, we have learned a new language — the dry, wild, disenchanted *argot* of the con-firmed and impenitent junkie. We have laughed at a kind of gallows-humour that eschews self-pity; we have lis-tened to a plethora of reminiscences, wry in tone and phrased with the most perceptive frankness; and we have heard — if we attended the Sixth Avenue presentation — some exemplary jazz, blown by the quartet of musicians who are among the guests at Leach's pad. Some of the characters are Negro, others Caucasian. The colour of their skin is of negligible importance. "The Connection" is probably the first American play of which this could be said. In a preliminary note, the author stresses that, although he envisaged some of the characters as white and others as coloured, "there need not be any rigidity in casting." This constitutes a minor, but vital, revolution.

I could pick one or two holes in "The Connection." For instance, it is sometimes guilty of repeating its effects; and with something approaching ferocity, it forbids us to admire any of its characters. But most of these minor flaws are inherent in the subject-matter — a way of life composed of recurrent lows and highs, all of which occur inside the nervous system and are seldom expressed in normal emotional relationships. Where Mr. Gelber overwhelmingly succeeds is in filling the stage with the kind of truth that goes beyond verisimilitude and achieves, at times, the robust, amoral candour of folk-poetry. As one of the squares keeps iterating: "That's the way it is. That's the way it really is."

"The Connection" seems to me the most exciting new American play that off-Broadway has produced since the war. It explores a frightening territory with clear, unprejudiced eyes, and a gift of words that makes its vision ours.

KENNETH TYNAN

THE CONNECTION

THE CONNECTION *was first performed on July 15, 1959 by The Living Theatre, directed by Judith Malina, with the following cast:*

Jim Dunn	Leonard Hicks
Jaybird	Ira Lewis
Leach	Warren Finnerty
Solly	Jerome Raphel
Sam	John McCurry
Ernie	Garry Goodrow
1st Musician	Freddie Redd
4th Musician	Michael Mattos
First Photographer	Louis McKenzie
Second Photographer	Jamil Zakkai
2nd Musician	Jackie McLean
3rd Musician	Larry Ritchie
Harry	Henry Proach
Sister Salvation	Barbara Winchester
Cowboy	Carl Lee

The play was designed by Julian Beck; the original tunes are by Freddie Redd and are available on Blue Note monaural LP 4027 and stereophonic LP 84027.

NOTE: The jazz played is in the tradition of Charlie Parker. There are approximately thirty minutes of jazz in each act. Its division within the act is a matter of pacing which can only be worked out on stage. The musicians use their own names throughout the play. In casting I think of Jim Dunn, Jack, Leach, Solly, Ernie and 2nd Photographer as Caucasians; Sam, Cowboy, Sister Salvation, Harry and 1st Photographer as Negroes. However, there need not be any rigidity in casting. In the original production Sam and Cowboy were Negroes.

ACT I

The players arrange themselves on stage a few minutes before the play begins. Solly is looking out of a window with binoculars. Behind him is a room full of homemade furniture. In center stage Sam is stretched out sleeping on a bed. Downstage left Leach and Ernie are slumped over a table. The 1st and 4th Musicians are at extreme right dozing at a piano. A small green light bulb hangs in the center of the room. A door to the toilet is rear left. There is, perhaps, a sign on the wall, "Heaven or Hell: which road are you on?" Perhaps there is a painting or an orange crate bookcase in the room. The house lights dim. Jim Dunn and Jaybird stroll up the aisle. They are wearing suits. Perhaps Jaybird has a darker shirt. They jump or hop on stage.

JIM:

Hello there! I'm Jim Dunn and I'm producing *The Connection*. This is Jaybird, the author. Hardly a day goes by without the daily papers having some item involving narcotics. Any number of recent movies, plays and books have been concerned with the peculiar problems of this anti-social habit. Unfortunately few of these have anything to do with narcotics. Sometimes it is treated as exotica and often as erotica. Jaybird has spent some months living among drug addicts. With the help of [name of director] we have selected a few addicts to improvise on Jaybird's themes. I can assure you that this play does not have a housewife who will call the

police and say, "Would you please come quickly to the [name of theatre]. My husband is a junkie."
(*House lights up.*)
Please turn the house lights down.

4TH MUSICIAN:

Hey, Jim, is Cowboy back?

JIM:

No, man, Cowboy is not back.
(*1st Musician plays his instrument hurriedly.*)

JIM:

Stop it kids. We haven't begun yet. I'm not finished. Turn those lights down.
(*Lights down.*)
Yes. We shall hear more from the musicians. A little better than that. That's what hooked me into this thing: jazz. I mean the music they try to stuff into movies and plays can't be called jazz. Not really. Tonight will be different.
(*Loses his place*)
When you're dealing with a taboo such as narcotics and trying to use the theatre in a way that it hasn't quite been tried before, you — I am taking a big gamble. Of course we are starting small. The [name of theatre] is small. I think playgoers should have some place to . . . you know what I mean.

JAYBIRD:

Jimmie, you're goofing. You've got your speeches mixed. What Jim is trying to say is that I am interested in an improvised theatre. It isn't a new idea. It just isn't being done. Remember: for one night this scene swings. But as a life it's a damn bore. When all the changes have been played, we'll all be back where we started. We end in a vacuum. I am not a moralist. However, some of you will leave this theatre with the notion that jazz and narcotics are inextricably connected. That is your connection, not —

JIM:

This word magician here has invented me for the sole purpose of explaining that I and this entire evening on stage are merely a fiction. And don't be fooled by anything anyone else tells you. Except the jazz. As I've said, we do stand by the authenticity of that improvised art. But as for the rest it has no basis in naturalism. None. Not a bit. Absol —

JAYBIRD:

This is getting embarrassing. We've gone through this. The improvising comes later.

JIM:

What I mean to say is that we are not actually using real heroin. You don't think we'd use the real stuff? After all, narcotics are illegal.

(*A knock. Everyone stiffens. Leach opens the door. Enter 2nd and 3rd Musicians.*)

2ND MUSICIAN:

Have we started yet?

JIM:

Emphatically not! Not until I'm finished. Dig?

2ND MUSICIAN:

What are you selling this time, Jim? Aren't you the

cat that was trying to sell me valve oil last week?

JIM:

I only asked you — oh, what's the use? Can't you do something?

JAYBIRD:

Why should I? Pay no attention to them. My primitive tribe is getting restless.

2ND MUSICIAN:

I have a gig for us. They're even going to pay us money.

JIM:

You see, I am taking a gamble. But why are salesmen put down? I'm selling an idea. What's so immoral about that?

2ND MUSICIAN:

Swing Baby. [1st Musician's name], we have to get some tunes prepared.

JIM:

Anyway, I was talking about the problem of naturalism. Did I say anything about that? Well, it's out of the question. Where could it lead? A sociologist's report on the pecking order of Bowery bums. No, out of the question. Right, Jaybird? Right.

JAYBIRD:

No!

(*House lights on.*)

JIM:

Again? What's happening backstage? Is everyone high before we start? Turn those damn lights off!

JAYBIRD:

I have had enough for now. Isn't it time to leave?
(*Exits into the audience. House lights down.*)

2ND MUSICIAN:

Please don't leave us! Please don't leave us!

JIM:

Why don't we do the whole play in the dark?
There's an idea for you, Jaybird.

JAYBIRD:

I've had enough of your ideas.

JIM:

Well, Jaybird did have some prepared things about
unions that I thought were pretty funny, but — I
shall return.

(*Exit Jim. Leach stands up and unfolds a tablecloth. He
snaps it and lays it out. With a large knife he starts cutting a pineapple. He has a handkerchief around a boil on
his neck.*)

LEACH:

I'm hungry. This is my place, why shouldn't I eat?
These people never eat. Don't they know it's nutri-
tious? Oh, this boil. Damn this boil. Dream world.
Narcotics. I live comfortable. I'm not a Bowery
bum. Look at my room. It's clean. Except for the
people who come here and call themselves my
friends. My friends? Huh! They come here with a
little money and they expect me to use my hard
earned connections to supply them with heroin.
And when I take a little for myself they cry, they
scream. The bastards. They wait here and make me

nervous. Sleeping. That's all they can do. Sleep. Last night I dreamt I was on a ladder. I wish Solly were awake. You know what I mean? He'd know. There were a hundred clowns dangling on this rope ladder, laughing to someone. You know what I mean? Then it was all a painting and the name psychology was written on the bottom.

(*Rapid entrance of Jim with 1st and 2nd Photographers. 1st Photographer is a Negro in a white suit, the 2nd Photographer white in a black suit. The 1st is swift and agile, the 2nd slow and clodlike. As the play unfolds they exchange, piece-by-piece, their clothing and personalities.*)

JIM:

I hope I haven't interrupted anything, Leach? I couldn't have. In keeping with our improvisation theme, I have an announcement. Have you been introduced to the cast?

LEACH:

Aw, Jimmie, I didn't want to wake anybody up.

JIM:

How kind of you. First things first. This is Leach.

LEACH:

(*Staring ahead and saluting*)
Yessir!

JIM:

This is Ernie. He's our dope-addict psychopath.
(*Ernie blows his mouthpiece.*)

JIM:

Solly? Wake up, Solly.

SOLLY:

> (*Raises his hand and waves*)
> Ad sum!

JIM:

> Sam is our expert in folk lore.

SAM:

> Don't fire until you see the whites of their eyes.

JIM:

> These are the musicians. I'm sure they need no
> introduction. This is [names all the musicians.]

(*1st, 2nd and 3rd Musicians stand, bow their heads, and
sit. The 4th Musician is asleep. Jim tugs at him.*)

4TH MUSICIAN:

> (*Reaching for his sleeve*)
> Cowboy here?

JIM:

> No, he is not. Now, friends —

1ST MUSICIAN:

> I can't tell the performance from the rehearsal.

JIM:

> Steady, boys, we have a long trip. Our other actors
> are off in the real world procuring heroin.

LEACH:

> Actors?

JIM:

> All right, junkies. During our trip we will incorpo-
> rate an allied art — the motion picture.

JAYBIRD:

(*From the audience*)
What?

JIM:

This is the ad lib part. Don't worry. Money! And, if everything goes right, you will be able to see the film version of this play. It was the only hip thing to do.

2ND MUSICIAN:

You're hip, my ass!

LEACH:

(*To Jim*)
Will you stop this cornball stuff.

ERNIE:

I knew they would pull something like this. I told you I didn't trust this cat!

JIM:

Come on, Jaybird. This can't go on like this.

JAYBIRD:

So far so good. Don't worry. Conflict!

JIM:

It just means more money. For you and for me. Besides, we aren't going Hollywood. They're making an avant-garde movie. The photographers know something about Griffith and Eisenstein.

LEACH:

You sure have to mention the right names.

SOLLY:

Leave him be.

JIM:

> Okay, you cats ought to smoke pot instead of using junk. It would make you more agreeable.
> (*Exit*)

ERNIE:

> (*To 1st Photographer*)
> How much they paying you, man?
> (*1st Photographer ignores him and moves in and about the stage with a light meter, framing with his fingers different parts of the set.*)
> What are you getting out of this, man?

2ND PHOTOGRAPHER:

> Oh, it'll pay the rent. Oh. Ah. Er. I'm visual, you see. I'm not able to express, ah, myself. Let's get the rest of the equipment. Ah.
> (*1st Photographer mentally adds up on his fingers, and they exit into the audience.*)

LEACH:

> Do you see that lightbulb? Do you realize that light travels at 186,000 miles per second per second? Solly, wake up. I want you to hear this.

SOLLY:

> (*Apparently asleep*)
> I haven't slept since the night I met you. Two years ago. But, for once, pretend that I am asleep.

LEACH:

> So, I was saying that light travels at 186,000 miles per second per second. You know what I mean? We, the human race, are being bombarded constantly with the light particles. And now the question is:

why aren't we dead? At 186,000 miles per second per second we should be annihilated. But we aren't. Why? I'll tell you. Man is transparent. You know what I mean? Man is transparent. Yes, transparent. That's why the light goes through him and doesn't hurt me or you. Now this is the interesting part. Are you listening, Solly?

(*Pause*)

If man is transparent, how do you account for his shadow? You know? To tell you the truth, I don't know the whole answer. You know what I mean? But I think that it has something to do with the alchemical nature of man. Got it? Some weird alchemical changes make the light's color different shades of black. Not too sure of that. Solly, what do you think of it? Does it have something to do with Indian philosophy?

SOLLY:

I'm hungry. What are you cutting to death today?

LEACH:

(*Places fruit on a dish*)
Hey, Sam, you want some pineapple?
(*Pushes Sam*)
Don't you want to eat?

SAM:

Now, man, you know I hate to be pushed. I have but one life. I'm waiting on Cowboy. What happened to Cowboy? And Leonard the Locomotive?

LEACH:

They ran off and got married! How do I know?

Go on, eat something.

SAM:

No, I's sick. Honest, I couldn't eat a thing.

LEACH:

Hey, Ernie! Wake up, boy! Time to eat. Huh? Here's some nourishment.

ERNIE:

Don't be a drag, man. Where's Cowboy and Leonard the Locomotive?

LEACH:

Cowboy, Cowboy. You rotten junkies. Is that all you can think about is dope? Dope? Dope?

2ND MUSICIAN:

Somebody call me?

3RD MUSICIAN:

(*To himself*)
My wife thinks I'm insane for doing this.

LEACH:

I'm offering you the fruit of the land. Cowboy is just going to kill you. I want to save you.

ERNIE:

Come off it, man. You steal so much shit from us that there are rumors of you opening a drug store.

SOLLY:

Sure, Leach is trying to turn on the whole world.

LEACH:

That's right. I'm saving all the heroin I can so that I can put it in vitamin pills. Can't you see everyone in the whole world being hooked without them knowing it?

(*Totters and laughs*)

Besides, I only take what's coming to me, and you don't have to come up here.

(*Crosses to 1st Musician*)

How about you, man? Pineapple?

(*1st Musician's head slowly falls and his body lapses into a deep sleep.*)

Hey, man. Pineapple?

1ST MUSICIAN:

(*Just before falling off his chair he straightens up*)

What's happening? What tune are we blowing? Cowboy back?

3RD MUSICIAN:

My wife thinks I'm insane.

LEACH:

No, Cowboy is not back.

2ND MUSICIAN:

Cowboy went to cop and got copped.

1ST MUSICIAN:

Oh.

(*Starts falling asleep again*)

1ST PHOTOGRAPHER:

(*In audience. Enthusiastically*)

That's the way it really is. That's the way it is.

SOLLY:

I'm hungry, Leach.

LEACH:

Okay.
(*Hands him the plate*)
Take the whole thing.

SOLLY:

Ernie, do you see where you make your mistake?
Ask and you shall receive.

ERNIE:

I'm not much for tact. I guess I'll never be.

SOLLY:

Well, man, it is a very rotting black shadow that
seeps through your body.

LEACH:

So you were listening? Maybe you know that
you're not the only one who thinks about these
things.
(*Holds his neck*)
My lousy boil!

SOLLY:

Put some hot water on it.

LEACH:

I think I will. Maybe I'll shave.

ERNIE:

(*To the audience*)
Cut your throat.

LEACH:

I've invited some chicks over. Jimmie thought it was
a good idea to put in a little battle of the sexes.
Where does he get his ideas? If anybody knocks

you take care of it, Solly. I don't feel like being arrested today. I haven't had dinner yet. Or my fix. (*Exits to toilet*)

ERNIE:

Hey, Solly, what were you talking about morals?

SOLLY:

Nothing much. I thought it would be easier if you pretended that Leach was a very good friend of yours. Let him think he's helping you.

ERNIE:

Oh. I thought you wanted me to follow the ten commandments or something.

SAM:

(*Reclining*)

Not a bad idea. I'm sick. Oh, powerful sick and hungry. I hope Cowboy gets back soon. I didn't like the idea of Leonard the Locomotive going with him. He's a practical joker. Every day he goes out. Or I go out. Or we're both way out. Every day. (*Sings*)

Sko-bah-dee. Skee-boh-dah. Same old stuff. (*Laughs*)

Yeah. Where is the old Cowboy? I remember when I got out of Quentin with the Cowboy a few years ago. We were walking down Broadway. (*Gets up and walks in place*)

We swore off of swearing anything off. That's the way it is — you know something in your mind for so long and you know that talking nonsense is just that and nothing more. Yeah, man, we were going to stay clean. Clean, man, clean. We collared the first connection we could find. I said, "What am I doing?" Just one fix won't hurt anything.

(*Starts jogging in place*)

What is this thing I'm fighting? That taste come back to your mouth. And that's what you want. That taste, that little taste. If you don't find it there you look some place else. And you're running, man. Running. It doesn't matter how or why it started. You don't think about anything and you start going back, running back. I used to think that the people who walk the streets, the people who work every day, the people who worry so much about the next dollar, the next new coat, the chlorophyll addicts, the aspirin addicts, the vitamin addicts, those people are hooked worse than me. Worse than me. Hooked.

(*Stops jogging and falls on the bed*)

SOLLY:

They are. Man, they sure are. You happen to have a vice that is illegal.

1ST PHOTOGRAPHER:

(*In audience*)

That's the way it is. That's the way it really is.

SAM:

I guess so. What am I talking about?

SOLLY:

You are fed up with everything for the moment. And like the rest of us you are a little hungry for a little hope. So you wait and worry. A fix of hope. A fix to forget. A fix to remember, to be sad, to be happy, to be, to be. So we wait for the trustworthy Cowboy to gallop in upon a white horse. Gallant white powder.

SAM:

There ain't nothing gallant about heroin, baby.

ERNIE:

Will you stop talking about it? You cats are a drag. It's getting on my nerves. I've got a job tonight and I've got to get straight.
(*Blows his mouthpiece*)
Why doesn't that bastard get here? He probably took all our money and burned us.
(*Knock.*)

LEACH:

(*Off stage*)
See who it is, Solly.

SOLLY:

(*At the window*)
It's Harry. He's got his suitcase.

LEACH:

(*Off stage*)
Let him in. I hope he doesn't want to stay here.
(*Solly opens the door and Harry walks in and looks around. Then he goes to the light socket in center stage and plugs in the cord of the portable phonograph. He opens the phonograph and puts on a Charlie Parker record — all in silence. The record plays for two minutes. Everyone assumes an intense pose of listening. Afterwards there is a silence and Harry carefully picks up the*

record, closes the phonograph, unplugs the cord, and leaves. There is a long pause. One of the musicians starts playing and the others join him in cementing their feelings. They play for about one minute.)

JAYBIRD:

(*Enters from the audience*)

Cut it! Cut it! You are murdering the play. What are you doing? Let's go over it again. You're to give the whole plot in the first act. So far not one of you has carried out his dramatic assignment.

(*Calms himself. Leach enters.*)

I had characters, with biographies for each of them. I thought that was clear. This is improvised theatre! And what have you provided? Do you think you are doing a slice of life?

SOLLY:

(*Shouting*)

Stop! Stop the action! Why did you seek out dope addicts? We didn't have to go through with this. Now quit complaining. Besides you've changed into a monster. Why don't you stay on stage with us?

JAYBIRD:

Never mind that now. There are to be no realistic body movements as we rehearsed. No longer is your hand your own hand. You are part of something infinitely larger. Solly, where is the philosophy I put into your mouth?

SOLLY:

It went up in smoke before the show.

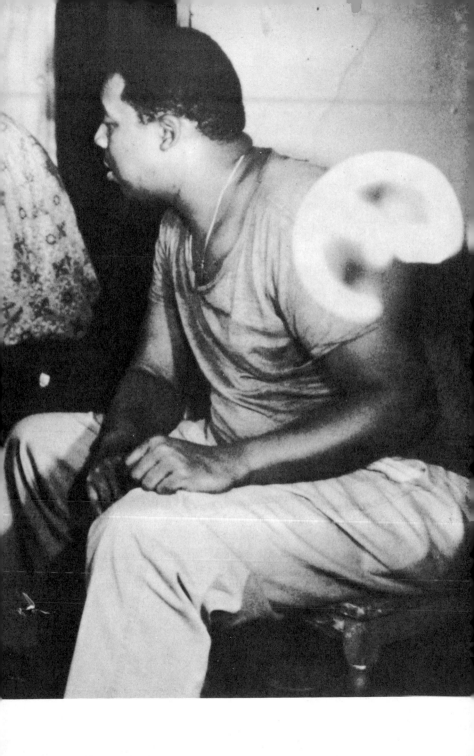

JAYBIRD:

A monster? I'm a monster? What do you know about the theatre?
(*Pause. Softly*)
Leach, where is the plot? Give it away, expose it, say it three times. Don't be anal.

LEACH:

I flushed it down the toilet.

JAYBIRD:

Sam, Ernie, is this a conspiracy? Where are your confessions? Your capsule comments?

ERNIE:

Where are my capsules?

SAM:

Man, you've been telling us to act natural. Now we don't own our own hands.

JAYBIRD:

You may know more about junk, but let me swing with this production. Okay, let's get on with it.

SOLLY:

Go ahead [name of 1st Musician], it's our stage now.
(*Jaybird exits into the audience to the jeers of those on stage. The musicians play for five minutes while the photographers move about the stage with their camera and glaring lights.*)

1ST PHOTOGRAPHER:

Take 27-A.

2ND PHOTOGRAPHER:

This is terrific stuff! I wonder how much will have

to be cut out of it? Terrific! Do you think we'll get a shot of the connection?

1ST PHOTOGRAPHER:

You mean Cowboy or Leonard the Locomotive?

2ND PHOTOGRAPHER:

No, no. I mean the man behind them. I mean the big connection.

1ST PHOTOGRAPHER:

If I were him I wouldn't want to show my face.

LEACH:

So you fellows want to see the man, the man behind the man.

2ND PHOTOGRAPHER:

Will he be here?

LEACH:

No, kiddies, he will not. I have been on this scene for a long, long time and I have never seen him. Sit down. Sit down. I have never seen the man because there is no man.

2ND PHOTOGRAPHER:

You mean there isn't any organized international setup?

LEACH:

No.

ERNIE:

Sure there is.

2ND PHOTOGRAPHER:

Then somebody must be the head of it.

ERNIE:

No, I don't think there's any head.

2ND PHOTOGRAPHER:

If you have an organization, somebody must be in charge. Hey, Sam, who's in charge?

SAM:

I am.

2ND PHOTOGRAPHER:

You are?

SAM:

Sure. I am the man as much as anyone. Listen, I am your man if you come to me. You are my man if I go to you.

2ND PHOTOGRAPHER:

Well, where does it start?

SOLLY:

Right here!

SAM:

Or over there.

2ND PHOTOGRAPHER:

I don't understand.

SOLLY:

(*At the window with binoculars*)
Nobody here understands that. They wouldn't be here if they were that interested. To us here it is a mystery where Cowboy goes. Anyone coming to Leach feels that he is the central actor in his own drama. An artifical and melodramatic organization.

But that is the setup. Surely it starts in the ground and grows up as a poppy. After that it is a mundane game for me, that is, for me.

1st PHOTOGRAPHER:

That's the way it is. Really, that's the way it is.

SOLLY:

The man is you. You are the man. You are your own connection. It starts and stops here. You come here to take pictures. And now you're getting involved at your own risk.

LEACH:

You think we ought to turn them on, Solly?

SAM:

I'm not donating anything.

LEACH:

I'm not asking you.

SOLLY:

Don't look at me. Ask them.

LEACH:

Well?

2nd PHOTOGRAPHER:

They say one shot and you can never stop. You're hooked.
(*Leach laughs*)

1st PHOTOGRAPHER:

You got any pot?

LEACH:

(*Laughs*)

Oh, this is the end. They send two square photographers. And one of them turns out to be a pot-head.

1ST PHOTOGRAPHER:

(*To 2nd Photographer*)
Marijuana.

LEACH:

Mari-juana. No, I don't have any pot. But how quaint of you to ask.

2ND PHOTOGRAPHER:

They say marijuana leads to the stronger stuff.

1ST PHOTOGRAPHER:

Shut up.

LEACH:

(*Pointing to the 1st Photographer*)
I'd like to turn that one on. He'd be crazy. I'd like to see that.

ERNIE:

No, I'd like to turn the other one on, and knock him out. Oh, he'd be helpless. At first, that is.

SAM:

You are certainly a mean bunch of boys.

LEACH:

Mind your own business.

SOLLY:

(*Looking out of the window*)
I can't see you. Yes, now you are in focus.

LEACH:

Is that Cowboy and Leonard the Locomotive?

SOLLY:

No, man, I'm looking for a woman.
(*Exit photographers into the audience.*)
Goodbye.

ERNIE:

I'm tired of waiting. Let's do something.

SOLLY:

Hello there! I'm the nineteenth century and I'm
producing the twentieth. Unfortunately, the twentieth century has developed anti-social habits. There
isn't a day that goes by without some item in the
daily papers involving insanity. We've gone out
and bribed a few natives. Actually, I'm the only
white man the natives trust. If we can start a small
opium war — I always wanted to start a war.

LEACH:

Cool it, Solly. Those cats make our living. Oh, my
neck. My boil!

SOLLY:

You're right. I've always wanted an audience, but
now I've got one. Imagine someone wanting to have
real junkies on stage. Wow! Believe me, we're not
here for the money.

ERNIE:

Speak for yourself.

SOLLY:

It's not that much. As you have gathered, we are,
as they say in the tabloids, dope fiends. We are
waiting. We have waited before. The connection is

coming. He is always coming. But so is education, for example. The man who will whisper the truth in your ear. Or the one who will shout it out among the people. I can't generalize and believe it. I'm not made that way. Perhaps Jaybird has chosen this petty and miserable microcosm because of its self-annihilating aspects. This tells us something about Jaybird, but nothing about me. Hurry, hurry, hurry. The circus is here. Suicide is not uncommon among us. The seeking of death is at once fascinating and repellent. The overdose of heroin is where that frail line of life and death swings in a silent breeze of ecstatic summer. The concept of this limbo you can hold in your palsied hand. Who else can make so much out of passing out? But existence on another plane is sought, whether to alleviate the suffering from this one, or to wish for death, it doesn't matter. I hate over-simplification. Sam! Sam is simple. Sam, someone, say something. Say something to the customers.

1ST PHOTOGRAPHER:

(*In audience*)
Man, that's the way it really is.

SAM:

Oh, man. I'm not much for this sort of thing.

SOLLY:

Pay your dues. Pay your dues.

SAM:

Okay. If that's the way it is. But who's to say? Who's there to squeeze the ball into his own shape

and tell me this is right. You know that. What does
Jaybird want? A soft shoe dance? I don't need any
burnt cork, you know. Now, Solly, you know
Leach. When you met him he came on with how
easy it would be to exist if you two shared expenses.
I remember you slept there. It was cheap. Little
rent, some food here and there whenever the bastard
felt like sharing what he had. Or Cowboy cooking
up a storm of food that he swiped in the super-
market. But Leach, man, Leach is a queer without
being queer. He thinks like a chick. You wouldn't
live with that. I certainly wouldn't. Sometimes I
wish he would stop fighting it and make the homo-
sexual scene. It would be easier on all of us. Besides,
he would swing more himself. Now he's undepend-
able, like a womans. He's like everybody's mother. Cowboy treats him like a womans and everything is fine. I can't do it. I just look at him, and I
can't do it. And there's Solly. Man, he's hard to
figure. Educated, shit, he knows an awful lot. But
then he's here waiting on the same stuff I am. And
he ain't rich. He don't get high unless he's happy.
I can never figure that out. Most cats get high when
they're down. Not him. Mostly I sees him in my
mind with dancing on the street. Yeah, dancing
down through the people. Sometimes yelling, sometimes whispering to people. Always with a book. I
don't remember ever seeing him on the street without a book. He watches everything. I was playing
with this hoop
(*Picks up hoop*)

and he tells me about the Roman's symbols of death
or some shit like that. He's always telling me what
I do is got to do with the Africans or the Navahos.
He breaks me up. A stand up cat. I like him.
(*Pause*)
Ernie?
(*Pause*)

ERNIE:

What do you want? Get us all busted?

SAM:

You don't want much. A little dope and your horn.
I don't trust you.

ERNIE:

The same.
(*Blows his mouthpiece*)

LEACH:

Your confession is next, son. Shut up. You think
it's easy?

SAM:

As long as Ernie is straight with me, I am with him.
But I don't like him. I hold back, you know? He has
no will power when it comes to not having anything to get high with. Hey, is there any beer left?

2ND MUSICIAN:

No.

LEACH:

My neck hurts. I'm going to put more hot water on
it.
(*Exits to toilet*)

SAM:

They have a saying in this world: It isn't the shit that will do you in, it's the lack of it. I can't put Ernie down too hard. I steal. But I steal from people I don't like, and I wouldn't touch a match stick of a friend of mine. Listen! I like telling stories best. I have quite a rep . . . repi . . . quite a lot of stories that would tickle the hairs on your ass. But I'm kinda sick right now. You can imagine. I mean, you've seen pictures of guys like me. It's torturous. Well, I'm coming off this here stage in a minute or so and I'll be in the lobby. I could use a little money.

(*Music begins softly.*)

Only till I get myself straightened out. I'm supposed to see this guy next week about working in a book store. Solly introduced me. Didn't you, Solly? Well, I'll be making a lot of bread then. I's sick, good people. I'll talk to you when I come offen this silly stage. I got some powerful stories in me when that shit flows in my veins. Right now I'm going to lay down for a minute. Maybe the music will help.

(*Musicians play for about five minutes.*)

ERNIE:

Trust me? Man, I don't care one way or the other. Sam's right about me in his own way — I only care to play. And . . .

(*Smile*)

. . . a little dope makes life enjoyable. I play the same — with or without it.

(*Blows his mouthpiece here, and throughout the speech*)

That's the truth. No square bullshitter is going to change me. That's for sure. I've had to hock my horn. Do you know what that feels like? I take the few measly pennies to some connection and get high. That's where my horn is now — the hock shop. I got a job tonight and no horn. Maybe someone will borrow me theirs. I don't know. I'm lonely! Not for you or anybody on this stage. I know these people. I've known them a long time. Too long.
(*Walks over to 2nd Musician*)
Can I use your horn tonight, man?
(*No answer*)
Did you see? Do you? Sam isn't too bad. He could of told some really rotten bits that people tell about me. Thanks, Sam.
(*No answer*)
They say I threw a kid out the window, after he took an overdose. Don't believe it.
(*Photographers enter and circle around Ernie.*)
Well, there's Leach. An orphan. Not too many people know that. Yeah, his old man was a musician. Died when he was eight. County authorities took him to a farm until he was seventeen. Poor kid. Bah! Leach went to work in a book store and one day he left with everything in the till and went to New York. He became a cheap businessman. He's always trying to be so hip. He still is just a petty conniving businessman. Leach has run away with the till from more cities and people than I'll ever know. Of course, Leach tells another story: he was cheated, he was insulted, he was dealing with squares, he

was . . . you know the story.

(*Smiles*)

So do I, for that matter. Get this straight. I admit when I've sinned. That's more than you will get from most.

VOICE:

Come off it.

ERNIE:

Who said that?

(*No answer*)

Money and sex. That's all I hear from you. So here it is right back. Leach, sexually speaking, can't be with a girl for more than one night. He likes the courtship. The playing up. The making out. Not it itself. You don't like hearing the truth, do you, Leach?

(*No answer*)

Leach uses junk that way. He doesn't enjoy junk, ever. I'm suspicious of people who never enjoy getting high. Oh, but he loves the excitement of getting it.

VOICE:

Come off it.

ERNIE:

Leonard the Locomotive? Cowboy? Hey, Solly, didn't that sound like Leonard the Locomotive?

(*No answer*)

He's crazy, that Leonard is. He must have been crazy about trains when he was a kid. He really thinks he's a locomotive at times. You photogra-

phers stop taking my picture! Where's Jim? We aren't being paid for being film actors.

(*Pause*)

Solly and Sam are very much alike. Surprise you? It's funny, in a way. They are of course very different people. Solly can read Greek and Hebrew.

(*Speaking progressively faster*)

I don't think Sam can read English. But they are the same. In this way. They swing with being high. Sam has been around junk and junkies all his life and no one is more familiar with that peculiar code that goes with it, you dig? He learned the hard way. Solly knows instinctively. I mean he was born hip. God knows why he's here. I tell everyone that he is just like that damned author who wrote this damned play. He just came around and acted like he was a junkie so that he could go home to his wife and kids and get us on paper. No, that was a bad act and everyone knew it. Not Solly. If he's acting then I'm fooled. And yet — well.

(*Toots mouthpiece. Starts again, slowly*)

Well, Sam is going to be around junk and junkies the rest of his life. He has no choice. Really. I don't feel that way about Solly. Both of them dig music. I mean they dig it. I mean they have an emotional digging. Which brings us to Cowboy. He's a good businessman. Some cats think he is a sweetheart. I mean he's noted for his honesty. I mean I hope he gets here soon, but he is the guy who will not run out. I think it's good business. Not a kind heart. After all, cross country gossip travels at high speed in my world. And nobody cheats him. And he used to blow [name of horn] like myself. I mean I still blow [name of horn] but he used to.

VOICE:

Come off it.

ERNIE:

Magic. That's what Cowboy does. I mean he makes something out of nothing. I've got the horrors. Where is Cowboy? Oh, he's fast with a knife. I saw him in action. I never believed it but there it was: knowing the danger before it happened. And then the quick move.

VOICE:

Come off it.

ERNIE:

Stop it. Shit! Shit! I don't trust any of you. Yes, I've tied everything into nice small packages for you. You can go home and say that Ernie really knows. Boy, he really can rip things apart. Shit. Do you hear? I don't trust one son of a bitch here or in the audience. Why? Because I really don't believe any of you understand what this is about. You're stupid. Why are you here? Because you want to see some-one suffer. You want to laugh at me? You don't want to know me. And these people? Sam doesn't care about me or my music when it comes right down to it. He's for number one — himself. Solly's young. Besides, he won't be a junkie all his life. He will be so far out of it he won't have to hear the rotten stories about his life being vomited up by thieves and misfits. It's Cowboy's business to screw me. And Leach? He wants to have me begging. He wants my guts out. I knew this would happen when I started talking. I knew it. I've tried. I just can't make it. I can't explain any more to you. I tried. A little anyway. I tried. My old man made me work on his farm every day until I was seventeen and never paid me a dime. All I got was a slap across the face for thanks. Where's Cowboy? Where is he? That bastard better come back. It's no use. No use. I want my money. Where is my pay? We're supposed to be paid. Jaybird, where's my pay? I'll kill you. Do you hear?

(*Starts off stage. Solly restrains him. Photographers exit. Jaybird leaves the theatre.*)

He's leaving, Solly. That's what the confession was for, wasn't it? Solly, he's leaving. We'll never get paid. I won't sign the confession. I won't sign! We'll never get paid. They made movies and it's no use. No use.

(*Sits down. Mumbles*)

No use. No use.

(*Silence 2nd Musician falls off his seat. He gets up and starts playing. The others join him for about five minutes of music.*)

ERNIE:

Give me a cigarette.

2ND MUSICIAN:

Let's split. No sense getting hung on a hanger. Cowboy got himself busted.

1ST MUSICIAN:

He'll be here. Let's stick.

3RD MUSICIAN:

My wife thinks I'm insane.

(*Sam gives him a cigarette. Ernie lights it and throws the match on the floor.*)

LEACH:

(*Enters and looks around. His boil still hurts*)

Who threw the match on the floor? What do you think I'm running here? A hotel for slobs? I feed you and even give you my clothes. And what do you do? Look at this place! Look at it! It's a pigsty. A pigsty. I just mopped the floor, too. Oh, what else could I expect?

(*Pause*)

Where's Cowboy?

(*No answer*)

Oh, my neck! Solly, what do you think I ought to do? Solly, Sam? Ernie, take a look at this. Will you?

(*Ernie examines Leach's neck.*)

ERNIE:

Looks bad, Leach. I'd see a doctor. I hope you might die. And listen: I threw the match on the floor. I want my money. I want out. Now.

LEACH:

What do you mean?

(*Turns suddenly and Ernie accidentally breaks the boil*)

Aaaaah!

(*Everyone except Solly runs to him. Leach is on the*

*verge of tears. Sam takes control of the situation and
puts Leach on the bed. Ernie, in disgust, stands next to
Solly at the window. Everyone calms down. Sam gets a
clean cloth and wraps it around Leach's neck. Leach
brushes everyone aside, picks up a mirror, examines his
boil, and then turns to Ernie.)*

Ernie, I'm a man of principle. I want you to pick
up that match and whatever else you've thrown on
the floor. Or get out.

ERNIE:

(*Pause*)

Man, I'm a musician. I blow my horn. I'm no god-
damn housekeeper. Not for you or anyone else.

LEACH:

I think you better leave.

ERNIE:

I'm waiting on the Cowboy. I got my bread in his
pocket. And I'm not leaving until I get my fix.

LEACH:

How many times have I turned you on? For nothing! How many times did you flop here? Have I
ever turned you out into the cold? Man, you're un-
grateful. You're selfish. And don't forget it.

ERNIE:

I'm going to vomit. Man, I can't take this. Give me
back my bread and I'll get out of here.

LEACH:

You didn't give me any money. Besides, I haven't
got any money.

1ST PHOTOGRAPHER:

> (*In audience*)
> That's the way it is. Man, that's the way it really is.

ERNIE:

> You've got enough on you. You always have enough on you. Miserly bastard. Like what happened to the dollar cap, to the three dollar bag? And that was some good shit, too.

LEACH:

> Man, you are living in another time. That was years ago. Don't blame me for what it costs.

ERNIE:

> Who else is there to blame? As far as I know you're just a screwball who is playing the small business-man.

LEACH:

> Get out! Get out! Why don't you stop pretending that you're a musician? Why do you carry that silly mouthpiece? Why? You're never going to use it. You can't play any more. You've got to practice, you dig?

ERNIE:

> What do I do now? Drop my pants and bend over? I'm waiting for Cowboy. And I'm not leaving until he gets back.

(*Solly picks up a chair and smashes it on the floor. Silence.*)

LEACH:

> What did you do that for?

SOLLY:

I hate petty arguments. Besides, Cowboy's coming.

LEACH:

What do you mean?

SOLLY:

Cowboy's coming.

LEACH:

Let me have the binoculars.
(*Pause*)
Who is that with him? It doesn't look like Leonard the Locomotive. Man, it's someone in uniform. It's the cops.

SOLLY:

No. No. It isn't any cop. Take another look.
(*Laughs*)

LEACH:

It's some kind of uniform. I don't like it. Who is it?

SOLLY:

It's some kind of salvation sister.

LEACH:

Are you sure?

SOLLY:

I'm not sure of anything. I think it's beautiful. Whatever Cowboy's up to certainly is good for a laugh.

LEACH:

What in the world is he doing with a salvation sister? Do you think he's going to bring her in here? He's crazy. Crazy! And what happened to Leonard the Locomotive?

JIM:

> (*Quick entrance with a cigarette with holder in one hand*)
> Hello again. Did you miss me, my charming audience? Ah, how sweet. Things are getting exciting around here. Don't you think so?

(*Photographers enter and move around him while he is thinking of what to say. He dismisses them with a movement.*)

> I am told that Leach has invited some lovely ladies to our little party. We shall see what we shall see. I may even convince Jaybird to come back.

ERNIE:

> Where's our money?

SOLLY:

> Cool it.
> (*To Jim*)
> You'd better come through. I'm not responsible for what Ernie will do.

JIM:

> Huh? Good people, do not be intimidated by any of these boys during the intermission. No matter what they tell you they will be turned on a scientifically accurate amount of heroin in the next act. And that is their payment for the performance, excluding the

money made on the movie. Also, we are selling some Turkish delight [and whatever else that is sold] in the lobby. Now . . . anyone in the audience for a smoke?

(*Lights slowly fade.*)

ACT II

(Music, then lights slowly up. As the music continues for about 5 minutes, the musicians take turns going into the toilet. As the last musicians exits, Ernie enters the toilet. Solly is sleeping at the window. Sister Salvation is looking around the room on tiptoe. Sam, on the center couch, begins to stir and the Sister "shshes" him. The music ends. Ernie enters, high, spots a chair and goes to it. Cowboy enters: he has a red bandana around his neck.)

COWBOY:

Sam?

SAM:

Coming, right now.

SISTER:

Shsh. You heard Brother Cowboy. There's a nice young woman next door that is very sick. Now please don't make any noise. One can say things in a tiny voice as well as a big one.

COWBOY:

Thank you, Sister Salvation. You are a great help to all of us.

SISTER:

Is there a bathroom, Brother Cowboy?

COWBOY:

Yes, mam. But Sam here hasn't had a bath in a long

time. I thought I'd help him wash away those sins of his. Understand?

SISTER:

Surely, Brother Cowboy.
(*Sam and Cowboy exit.*)
   (*To Ernie*)
   You look very pale, son. Is something the matter? Hungry, son?

ERNIE:

Leave me alone. I'm in no mood for conversation.

SISTER:

Soul. Yes, my dear child, the soul. I'm sure of it.

ERNIE:

You have invited yourself to a den of vipers, Sister Salvation. I'm sure you will find enough sins crossing your path today. So leave me alone.
(*Cowboy enters.*)

COWBOY:

Understand this, Brother Rat, Brother Sun and Brother Eel! Leonard the Locomotive and I met this fine woman just one mile from our home. You know where the central police station is? Not far from there, under a flag symbolizing American freedom of speech and religion, I stopped to hear the words of the Lord.

SISTER:

Amen.

COWBOY:

Amen. A few gentlemen we know began a conversation with me. They asked the all important questions. Where were you? What have you been doing? How was the rodeo and horse tricks? Leonard the Locomotive succeeded in attracting some attention with his famous locomotive yell, and this worker of the Lord . . .

SISTER:

Amen.

COWBOY:

. . . this worker and I engaged in a most enlightening discussion. We took a quiet walk home and I invited her up for a little tea.

LEACH:

Orange Pekoe.

COWBOY:

Possibly she, Leonard the Locomotive, and the power of the Lord saved us all. For the moment, that is.

SISTER:

Amen to that, Brother Cowboy.

COWBOY:

Amen, Sister Salvation. Now excuse me please.
(*Exit*)

SOLLY:

Sister Salvation, Sister Salvation, when did your record of saving souls start?

LEACH:

Cool, cool water, Solly.

SOLLY:

Have a little trust in the Lord, friend.

SISTER:

Brother, I began in the service of the Lord fourteen
years ago. But I have only been active these past
seven. If you could see the hundreds of faces smile
and light up when someone holds out a helping hand
to show the path of salvation, it would warm your
heart. You haven't known joy until you have seen
the way to God.
(*Pause*)
Do you know Harry McNulty?

LEACH:

We don't know anyone.
(*Cowboy enters.*)

COWBOY:

Excuse me, Sister Salvation. Solly, you're next.

SISTER:

There's something crazy going on.

SAM:

(*Following Cowboy*)
Save yourself, you sinners! Brother Cowboy has
some potent medicine made from the rarest, finest
witch doctor white flower that ever grew.
(*Laughs*)
Shiiiit. Oh, excuse me, Sister Salvation.

COWBOY:

Leach, how about making Sister Salvation a nice cup of tea while you're waiting.

LEACH:

I'm waiting to get on. Man, I'm sick.

SOLLY:

(*At the toilet door*)
I don't take long. Start the tea, I'll finish it.
(*Exits with Cowboy*)
(*Ernie starts playing "There is a Fountain Filled with Blood" on his mouthpiece. Then he starts singing it. After a few lines the words disappear and he is scat singing. Sister Salvation claps her hands in time and everyone joins her. The photographers enter from the audience.*)

SISTER:

Oh, it is good, good, good to hear such young men appreciate songs like that.
(*Notices the photographers*)
Who are they? Where did they come from?

LEACH:

They're all right. Friends of the family. Did Jay-bird come back?

1ST PHOTOGRAPHER:

Not yet.

SISTER:

What's a nice Negro boy like you doing here?

SAM:

I've seen the light!

(*Melodramatically*)

Yes, I've seen the light! Brethren, I used to be a sinner! A sinner!

(*Leach and Ernie laugh. Photographers exit.*)

A sinner that done bad to his fellow man. But now! Praise the Lord!

SISTER:

Amen.

SAM:

I am redeemed! From my eternal suffering I am redeemed! Like a pawn ticket.

(*Laughter.*)

I want to take the opportunity to thank each and every kind, gentle and good contributor in the audience. You have helped a most noble cause, and a cause that is dear to our hearts. That goodness, that goodness that flows in our veins is the evidence — is the evidence of our gratitude toward you and every one of our fellow men.

SISTER:

Amen.

LEACH:

I'm not on yet.

SAM:

You, too, Brother Eel, will be saved by Brother Cow in just . . .

(*Solly enters with Cowboy.*)

Ah, you see before you with your very own eyes Brother Sol. Hello, Brother.

SOLLY:

You weren't kidding, Sambo. This is powerful medicine. I'm going around and will become butter any minute.

SAM:

I should wash your mouth out with soap.

SISTER:

Amen. Amen. Are you through in the bathroom, Brother Cowboy?

(*Exit Leach.*)

COWBOY:

There is just Brother Leach, mam. And then our baptism will be all over.

(*Exit Cowboy.*)

SISTER:

That's all right, Brother Cowboy. You just keep working.

(*2nd Musician falls to the floor and 1st Musician helps him up. Sister Salvation starts over to him, but Solly interrupts her.*)

SOLLY:

Praise the Lord!

SISTER:

Amen.

SOLLY:

Sister Salvation, I want you to see the light. I mean, man, light travels at 186,000 miles per second per second. I'd like to see that, too. Watch it closely.

Faster and faster around your head. Now let your eyes cross. The light is forming an enormous circle around you. You're not helping me, baby. Help me. (*Starts to fall. Sam catches him and carries him to his seat*)

Mercy on me. I falleth before the Lord. Oh, man, it is too tiring. Man, whew! Where do all those sinners get the energy to be saved? Fantastic. I couldn't make it. You have to hand it to them. Day after day, trudging and pulling, they seek out energetic sinners. Each of them is saved ten or twenty times. It's just too much.

SAM:

You got to let yourself go. When you feel it inside, just let yourself go and wail.

SOLLY:

Man, I feel it inside, but I can't move. I'm stoned. (*Sits at window*)

SISTER:

(*To Ernie*)
Where do you come from, son?

ERNIE:

(*Almost asleep*)
What?

SISTER:

Are you all right, son?

ERNIE:

Yeah. Sure. Of course, baby, I'm all right. Where

do I come from? See, I can remember.

SISTER:

Yes. Where do you come from?

ERNIE:

California.

SISTER:

That's marvelous.

ERNIE:

What's so marvelous about it?

SISTER:

It's so clean and healthy there. The trees, and everything is so green.
(*Pause*)
I thought perhaps — perhaps you know Harry Mc-Nulty. He's Irish.

ERNIE:

Yes.
(*Falling asleep*)
It is. Green.
(*Falls out of the chair. Sister Salvation helps him up and Cowboy comes over and slaps him gently.*)
I'm all right. Man. Leave me alone. It's green. I want to sleep.

COWBOY:

The poor boy hasn't slept in days.

SISTER:

Oh, we better leave him alone. He looks like a good prospect to save.

COWBOY:

Why don't you make yourself a nice cup of tea.
(*Sister Salvation exits.*)

LEACH:

I'm not even high. I don't feel a thing. I don't feel
a thing.

SAM:

If you don't feel a thing, man, then you're higher
than any of·us.

LEACH:

You gave them more. How much did you give
Ernie, Cowboy? He's knocked out. And I don't
feel a thing.

COWBOY:

Cool it. You know Ernie has been chipping. I gave
him the same as you, but you got a higher tolerance. Dig?
(*Photographers enter from the audience.*)

2ND PHOTOGRAPHER:

I . . . I don't know how to say this.

COWBOY:

I don't know you, man. Who are you?

2ND PHOTOGRAPHER:

I'm here to do the film.

LEACH:

Jim sent him. But weren't you the one that was so
afraid? Yeah. What about the other photographer?

1ST PHOTOGRAPHER:

> Count me out. I don't want nothing to do with this.

LEACH:

> (*Laughs*)
> This is going to be fun. Cowboy, give him a taste.

COWBOY:

> Not out of mine.

LEACH:

> Out of mine. Go ahead, give him a little taste.

COWBOY:

> Are you sure you want to go through with this?

2ND PHOTOGRAPHER:

> (*Mumbles*)
> Yes.

JAYBIRD:

> (*Enters from the audience*)
> Okay. Okay. Aren't you carrying this too far? What is happening here? You aren't here to do this sort of thing. Destroy yourself, but this wasn't in our deal.

COWBOY:

> Jaybird, I don't want to initiate anyone into the club. This boy is asking for it. You stop him. I'm too tired to talk.

JAYBIRD:

> I don't like it. It's not supposed to work this way. I've given you latitude. But this is too much.

LEACH:

Hey, Jaybird, you've never made it. Why don't you find out what it's all about before you put it down.

JAYBIRD:

Me? No. Not me. Never. Me?

LEACH:

You're supposed to know all about it. I mean this all is a play, man. It's not really real.
(*Snicker*)
Hey, I want to watch.

COWBOY:

Let's not talk here.
(*Smiling*)
You stay, Leach. Come on back.

(*Exit Cowboy, 1st Photographer and Jaybird.*)

LEACH:

So Jaybird will take a little taste for himself.

SISTER:

(*Enters. Walks to the window*)
Where are all those people coming from? Who are they? I don't see anybody out there.
(*Uses binoculars*)
I don't see anyone out there at all. This is very confusing.
(*To Solly*)
Do you know Harry McNulty?

SOLLY:

No. There are some questions I can't answer. That's one of them.

SISTER:

[Gives a short description of actor who plays Harry]

SOLLY:

What makes you think I would know him?

SISTER:

Oh, he loves jazz music. I thought perhaps . . . never mind, I'm probably wrong anyway. The Lord willing, that is.

(*2nd Musician falls off his seat. 1st Musician mechanically picks him up.*)

1ST PHOTOGRAPHER:

That is the way it is. Really, it is that way.

SAM:

Yes, it is. As long as we are talking religion, I got one that happened not too long ago.

(*To the musicians*)

You know Abdul the drummer? Well, Abdul is from Harlem and he has taken up the Moslem faith. A religious man if I ever saw one. Is there any beer?

2ND MUSICIAN:

No.

SAM:

One night Abdul and Cowboy and me were looking for some small connection. No luck anywhere. Everybody is tearing their hair out. Cowboy and I decide to try to score outside the city. Abdul gave us some money and told us to meet him at his pad. We go outside the city and score and everything is crazy. It is getting light out by now and we hurry back to

town and go to Abdul's pad. We knock. No answer.
Knock again. No answer. Cowboy tries the door
and it's open. We go in and there is Abdul in his
underwear kneeling on this rug and he got his hands
clasped together and eyes is tight shut. I say, "Abdul, we're back." No answer. "Abdul, baby, everything's cool. We made it." Still no answer. Cowboy
tries to stop me from talking to him because Cow
figures it must be important if Abdul won't even
turn around. We sit down. I can't stand the silence
any more. So I say, "Abdul, what the hell you
doing, man? Do you know who I am? What are
you doing on your knees, baby?" He turns around
and stares at me. Finally, he says, "Man, I was
praying that you would come back and turn me
on!"

SISTER:

(*Pause*)

That's a wicked story! Such language!

LEACH:

(*Enters*)

Here's your cup of tea, Sister Salvation.

SISTER:

Thank you, brother.

(*Cowboy enters with 2nd Photographer and Jaybird.
Jaybird has Cowboy's red bandana around his neck,
1st Photographer exits to the audience. 2nd Photographer
takes Sister Salvation's cup and sits.*)

COWBOY:

> Well, what's been happening? Sister Salvation, the bathroom is yours.
> (*Sister exits*)
> What have you been doing to that chick? I don't want her to leave with a suspicious thought in her head.

LEACH:

> You shouldn't have brought her here. I think she knows what's happening. Or she doesn't know and wants to.

COWBOY:

> There were two narcotic bulls on my back. Leonard the Locomotive went one way, and they followed him. I left with her. Man, it was close. I was about to throw the shit away.

SAM:

> What happened in there?

COWBOY:

> What a miserable sight it was. A night for comedy. I think Jaybird is pretty sick.
> (*Pointing to the 2nd Photographer*)
> He is.

LEACH:

> He's out of his skull. Look at him. Hey, man, how do you feel?

2ND PHOTOGRAPHER:

> Don't be a drag, man.
> (*They all laugh.*)

JAYBIRD:

I've got to lie down.

LEACH:

Go ahead! There's a bed.

JAYBIRD:

No, not here.
(*Whispers*)
There are too many people around. Wait a minute.
I'm sick.
(*Exits to toilet*)

SISTER:

(*Entering*)
Drink!
(*Backs up Jaybird. Jaybird runs into toilet, holding his mouth*)
That's what you've been doing in there!

COWBOY:

What do you mean, Sister Salvation?

SISTER:

What do you mean, Brother Cowboy? There are at least ten bottles of wine in the bathroom. All empty. Oh, Lord, before my very own eyes I have been deceived. Wine is a mocker, strong drink is raging: and whosoever is deceived thereby is not wise.
(*The following dialogue is underscored with the bass playing with Solly, and the horn with Sister Salvation.*)

SOLLY:

A false balance is an abomination to the Lord; but a just weight is his delight.

SAM:

Swing!

SISTER:

Be not among winebibbers, among riotous eaters of flesh. For the drunkard and glutton shall come to poverty. Who hath woe? Who hath sorrow? Who hath babbling? Who hath wounds without cause? Who hath redness of eyes? They that tarry long at the wine. They that go to seek mixed wine. At last it biteth like a serpent and stingeth like an adder.

SOLLY:

Who invented that uniform?

SISTER:

What?

SOLLY:

Who invented the uniform you are wearing?

SISTER:

I don't know. What has that got to do with it? It isn't what I was talking about. You can't get out of this that easily. You will pay . . .

SOLLY:

Foggy day in London, London, London town. It's the War Congress. 1878. Winter. The flock is assembling. Coming back to you now, Sister Salvation? Elijah Cadmen stood up and said, (*sotto voce*) "We need a military type uniform. War to the teeth and salvation to the world."

SISTER:

I thought that General Booth invented . . . I could

look it up in the library. Where did you learn these things? You would like our library. It's open to the public.

SOLLY:

Your bonnet was invented by the General's wife. There will be equality of the sexes, they scream. Dress shall be according to climate. 1880. International meeting. Fur caps in the Arctic. Veils in India. All embracing salavtion.

SISTER:

I give up. I give up. Stop.

SOLLY:

Don't surrender now. Or do. It was just, just, just, just one of those things.

SISTER:

What's a nice young man like you doing here? (*Laughter by all.*)

I don't understand. Why do you . . .? (*Laughter by all.*)

SOLLY:

No more war. You had better leave while the spirit of brotherhood prevails.

SISTER:

I don't want to leave. I know I'm a burden. I went to see about my funeral. The man at Morgen's funeral parlor said it would cost three hundred dollars for opening and closing the grave. Eighty-five dollars for the head stone. I'm growing old and my eyes are going. I don't want to leave. I've been in the hospital. They put the needle in my arm, too.

SOLLY:

Cowboy?
(*Nods to him*)
Go ahead, Sister Salvation, before we tell you who Harry McNulty is.

SISTER:

(*Cowboy takes her to the door*)
You are not alone. You are not alone.
(*Exit*)
You are not alone.

JAYBIRD:

(*Enters from toilet*)
Glad to have met you?
(*Laughs and sits down to sleep*)
(*The musicians play for about ten minutes. When finished there is a pause. Jim enters, taking notes.*)

JIM:

Leach? Leach? Where are the chicks? Where are the chicks?

LEACH:

Oh, man, my job was to invite them. I didn't guarantee anything. They'll probably show up. Hold your pants.

COWBOY:

Hey, man, are we getting any extra money for being in this movie scheme?

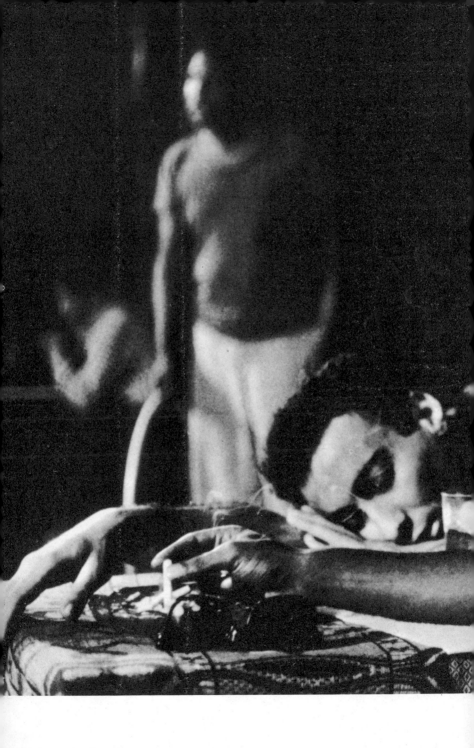

JIM:

You would have.
(*Pointing to 2nd Photographer*)
He isn't going to make any movies so far as I can see.

COWBOY:

Do I detect a note of hostility?

JIM:

No. No, but it wasn't right for you to give these people dope. Look at Jaybird. Oh, Jaybird!

COWBOY:

I didn't want to give either of them anything. It's their own responsibility. Man, they're old enough to know what they're doing.

JIM:

Okay. All right. I'm not a moralist. But we should get the chicks here. Oh, it didn't have to be chicks. Homosexuals would do. Some kind of chorus. I should have seen to it myself. You people are so unreliable.

JAYBIRD:

(*Mumbles*)
It's out of my hands! It's out of my hands! There is this wall between you and me, Jim. So that's what it does!

JIM:

I want a good show too. Is that too much? You know it's every penny I've got. You can't go on amusing yourself! Get girls or something. I'm telling you that'll do it, man.

LEACH:

Maybe you would like to turn on, too. Since you're not a moralist.

JIM:

No.
(*Points to his head*)
I've got a brain. Why are you cats really here?

LEACH:

It's fun.

SOLLY:

The money.

ERNIE:

It's something to do.

COWBOY:

Because we all love you.
(*Jim exits.*)

LEACH:

I'm not high, Cowboy.

COWBOY:

Wait awhile, man. Don't hurry it. Enjoy it, baby.

LEACH:

I didn't get a flash, Cowboy, I didn't get a flash.

COWBOY:

(*Laughs*)
It's been ten years since I've had a flash. Just sit down and look at a picture book.
(*Ernie blows his mouthpiece.*)
Not while I'm around. No, no. Practice in your

bathroom. Hey, Solly, what did your White Sox
[or any current sports reference] do today?

SOLLY:

The Yankees [or any appropriate sports reference]
beat them. Again. There's the worst habit I know
— the congenital losers.

COWBOY:

It's only a game. How did that new shortstop do?

LEACH:

You square bastards! Square daytime bastards. Base-
ball ain't hip.

SAM:

I ain't hip. Do you call it hip spending half the time
in jail?
(*Nods*)

LEACH:

They haven't got me yet.

COWBOY:

You better expect it. Besides, what's wrong with
day jobs? Or being square? Man, I haven't anything
against them. There are lousy hipsters and lousy
squares. Personally I couldn't make the daily work
scene. I like my work hours as they are. But it
doesn't make me any better. No, man, no.

LEACH:

You know what I'd do if I had a day job? Man, I'd
work about six months and then establish credit.
You know what I mean? Then I'd get every charge

card there is. Food, liquor and travel. Man, I'd go
all over the world. What could they do? Throw me
in debtor's prison? Not in America. No sir, we're
free here. You know what I mean? Man . . .

COWBOY:

What movies you been watching?

LEACH:

Others have done it.

COWBOY:

Seems like a lot of work. An awful lot of work.
Could you work six months? At what?
(*Sings*)
I'm dreaming of a white Christmas, just like the
ones I used to know.
(*Says*)
You know we live in a white society. Did you ever
see black snow?

SAM:

(*Wakes up*)
Who said snow?

SOLLY:

I've seen brown heroin from Mexico.

COWBOY:

But that's Mexico.

LEACH:

I'm not high, Cowboy, I'm not high.

COWBOY:

Give it time. Go eat something. Read a picture

book. Man, walk outside and let life —

MAN:

> (*In audience*)
> I gave Sam five bucks and I want a story. I want a story from Sam.

COWBOY:

> Who said that? Stand up.

MAN:

> (*Stands*)
> I want a story.

COWBOY:

> Insistent bastard.
> (*Takes hoop and wakes Sam*)
> Here, man, roll out some kind of jive. It's that cat there. Did he give you five?

SAM:

> Yeah. Can't you see that someone gave me five?

COWBOY:

> Then tell him a story.

SAM:

> (*Intermittently scratching his face and body*)
> Three, four years ago: let's see, there was me and the Cowboy and Leach. Yeah. Leach was selling books downtown. He always walked out of that store with one under his coat. Cowboy and he had a pad down near the waterfront. Me? I was scuffling. As usual. The point is we were very hot. I don't know whose fault that was. Leach can be loud.

Scream like a bitch in heat. Of course, Cowboy's and my record speak for itself. Anyway, what I last remember how it first began. Shiiit. Is that what I wanted to say? Man, this is very nice stuff. Anyway, there was a party. Leach was bribing this hustler with good old heroin. Funny thing, Leach always seems to have a place. If he and I have the same amount of money, I wind up on the street and he always got a weird kind of joint with foolish signs all around. This party. Did I tell you about the party? Kelly was there. He had his harem, too. That was when we called Kelly "Upsidedownface!" He didn't like it. He did have that kind of head. But, he always had three or four chicks with him. And did he like them go-go pills! Man, he took thirty or forty benzedrine a day. And believe me, I was brought up to believe that it was best to have just one man and one bitch in bed at the same time. But Upsidedownface wouldn't be satisfied with less than two and usually more. Maybe that's got something to do with him hanging himself. I don't know. That night one of his chicks was taking the trouble to bring me beer and to rub up against me. Man, she was a beautiful animal. Oh! Well, she was hung up in her head like everyone else I know. She kept talking about how she always wanted to marry a Negro. She came from the South or something. She kept calling me her Black Prince. Well, I don't care what a bitch say with her mouth. It's what she say with her body that has got my eye. Upsidedownface is a generous person. If you let him announce

to everyone what you can take away from him. You dig? While he was announcing the departure of the chick from his harem, the phonograph was playing and Leach was arguing with this bitch he invited. I think he was kissing her breasts or something. What made it an argument was that there were so many people around. Prostitutes sure can have prissy morals. The woman next door started complaining, knocking on the walls. Finally she came over. Leach told her off. About ten minutes later the cops knock politely on the door. They come in. What's going on here? Who rents this apartment? What's your name? and yours? Those sort of questions. We all played it cool. No searching. Nothing like that. The party went on. Not the same. The cops shake everyone. But, in a curious way, most cops and junkies are alike. Sado . . . Solly, sado what?

SOLLY:

Masochist.

SAM:

Anyway, we wondered if they would come back. People left, the music stopped. Leach started bitching. He felt insulted that everyone was going. The cops didn't come back. About a week later to the day we three were in the pad again. Cowboy cooked dinner that night. Ham. And peas. Yeah. We were finished eating and Leach was teaching me how to play chess. Which meant that he was playing with himself. He moved all the pieces and I would sit back and stroke my chin and say, "Yeah. Yeah."

Cowboy was reading some kind of hot book. The phone rings and it is some chick that doesn't particularly knock Leach out. But he gives a story and makes a date. I suppose this was to make Cowboy and me jealous. Leach has a funny mind. He tell us that he will be back at eleven o'clock. Sure. After he leaves, Cowboy pulls out some marijuana and we get high and have a few laughs about Leach. I was going to sleep.

(*Footsteps offstage, coming and going.*)

On the wall that I was looking at was a painting in orange and red, circles and lines. They began moving out of the painting and in my head, you know what I mean? Next thing I know the door is knocked down and these two guys with guns are over Cowboy and me. Wham! We're thrown against the wall. Well, this is old stuff in a way. If that sort of thing can ever be old stuff. First there is the scare. A few wacks and threats and we are supposed to tell all. All? Actually, Cowboy and I didn't know Leach had hidden about a quarter of an ounce in the couch. The greedy bastard! Then something funny happened. It seemed that they were after Leach. They looked at our arms. They could have thrown us in jail for those long snakes of old needle marks. Or they could have claimed that it was our stuff that they had found. But no. For some reason they know that Leach rented the apartment and they wanted him. Perhaps they thought he was the King of the Junkie World. That's what the papers call every squirt that is caught. Cowboy tells them that we are supposed to meet Leach in a certain bar not too far. Meanwhile, it is getting very close to eleven o'clock. They fall for it and we leave and start walking up the block. Arm in arm, of course. Leach is walking straight towards us. He's got this chick with him. Cowboy drops his cigarette and bends down to get it. While the cops are watching him, I raised my hand to my mouth. Leach got the idea, and kicks the chick who is about to scream hello to us. They walked right by. We didn't see Leach for two years. Heard he went to Texas, or some place unfit for humans. Anyway, we go into this candle-lighted bar and the Cowboy looks very carefully at everyone. The cops hurry him up. So Cowboy gets mad and picks out a rather well-tailored look-ing kid. Bing! They collar him, and take him along with us to the station. That poor kid screamed all the way down to the station and they put him in the observation room. They let us go. I don't know if they ever let that kid go. Man, that was a long one. I'm tired.

(*Mumbles and stretches, then sits*)

JAYBIRD:

(*Stands. Scratches face and body*)
You cats are actors?

COWBOY:

I'm not acting. You should have thought about that when you hired us.

JAYBIRD:

I'm not angry. Just amused. All you do is talk, talk,

talk. Is there no end to this babbling?
(*Calms himself*)
This part was to be blood and guts drama. It's not
for me that I plead with you. Think of the audience. Jimmie thinks of the audiences. I dream about
them. So far one would think this was a drawing
room comedy. If you were in the audience you'd
know what I'm talking about. Listen, I researched
everything carefully. I lived among you. Now what
are you doing? You've all changed. Man, you aren't
supposed to change. Just act naturally. Is that all
you know — destruction? I know better. Maybe it's
the audience. It's that? They're making you nervous.
They're making me nervous. Maybe we should
have tried it without an audience the first few
nights.
(*Starts to fall asleep*)

COWBOY:

It's not the audience, Jaybird.

JAYBIRD:

Don't feel inadequate. After all, I have a prison record too. We've all been in the army. We're veterans,
you and I. We're veterans.
(*Laughs*)
(*Ernie blows his mouthpiece.*)

COWBOY:

I feel great, don't you, man?

JAYBIRD:

I don't know . . . I don't know what's happening to
me.

(*Wearily*)

I do know that there isn't any hero in this play. I wrote a play with four heroes. Didn't I explain that part? You are all heroes. I mean in the theatrical sense. Cowboy, can't you act like a hero? It's the basis of Western drama, you know. Can't you make an heroic speech? You have not been upstaging it, at all. Look what you've done to the cameraman. Where's the other photographer?

(*1st Photographer enters from audience.*)

We want some angle shots of Cowboy. Our hero.

(*2nd Photographer wakes up and wobbles around Cowboy with 1st Photographer.*)

Cowboy, you can do for the show, Cowboy. We're all together. Say something.

COWBOY:

It's too much risk going out and scoring every night. I mean I'm followed every night and I have to scheme a way of getting back here. I'm tired. Man, I've been moving my whole life. You think I enjoy leaving love behind? I haven't anything to say. Is that what you wanted, Author?

(*To the photographers*)

I'm sick of the sight of you fake beboppers.

(*He takes hold of the 1st Photographer and pushes him to the end of the stage*)

Get out of here! I'm sick of the sight of you.

(*To the author*)

Sit down and quit worrying about your precious play. Sit down, Mother. Damn it! You can't find anything out about anything by flirting with people. What do you think we live in, a freak show? You be the hero. Relax, we won't run out on you. You're just high.

LEACH:

(*Softly at first*)
I'm not high. I'm not high at all. You know what I mean? I want more. Cowboy? Cowboy? You have some left. I'm not high. It's mine, Cowboy. Strictly speaking, it's mine and I want some more. Everybody's high and I'm not. You didn't give me as much as you gave them.

COWBOY:

Now, baby, why should I want to cheat you?

LEACH:

I want more.

COWBOY:

Man, you are high. That shit is in your system.

LEACH:

I want more.

COWBOY:

Okay, it's your life.
(*Exit Cowboy. Musicians play. Cowboy enters and gives Leach a small package. Leach performs the ritual of fixing and taking the heroin. No one pays any attention to him. He falls, dropping the "works."*)

COWBOY:

There goes my last spike!

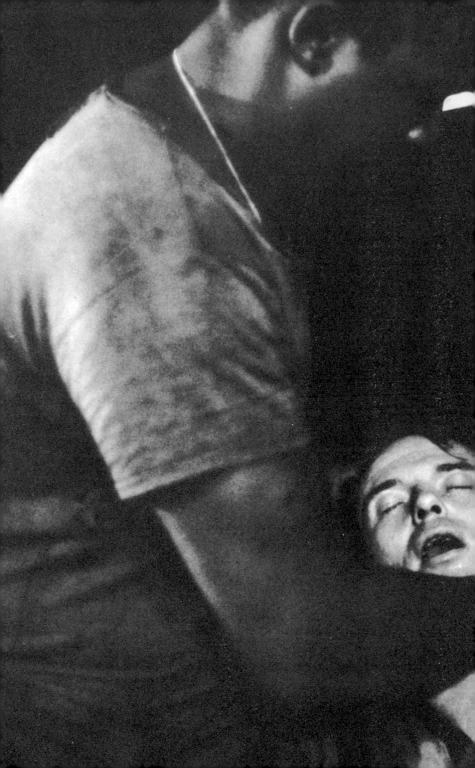

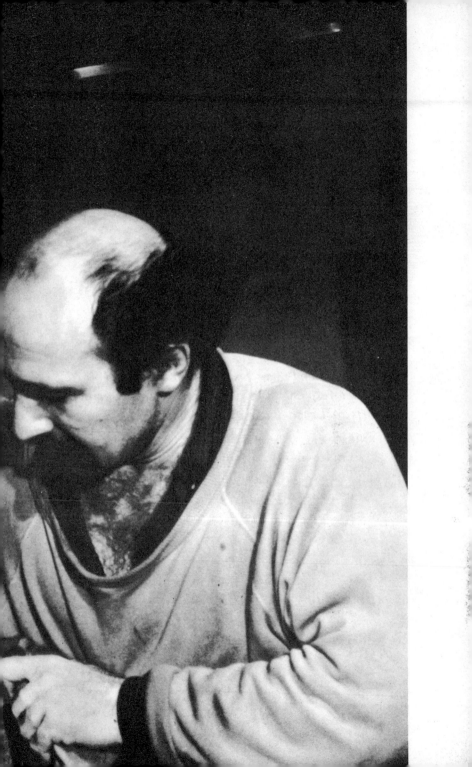

(*Goes to Leach. He realizes Leach has taken an overdose*)

Sam!

(*Sam slowly goes to him. One by one the musicians stop playing. Cowboy and Sam bring Leach to the couch. Cowboy starts artificial respiration.*)

2ND MUSICIAN:

Give him a salt shot.

COWBOY:

That was my last spike.

3RD MUSICIAN:

Let's pack up.

4TH MUSICIAN:

Let's get to that gig.

(*Cowboy and Sam walk Leach back and forth. He doesn't respond. They lay him on the couch. Jaybird starts to Leach but stops and sits again.*)

ERNIE:

I'm leaving. I don't like it. You know what I mean? I've got a gig tonight. I've got to find a horn to use. You dig?

2ND MUSICIAN:

Can we help?

SAM:

No, you might as well make that gig.

(*Ernie exits.*)

Chicken shit!

(*Musicians exit, each saying: "We'll see you tomorrow, Cowboy."*)

Later on, gentlemen, later on.
(*Looks at Solly*)
Why don't you go, too?

SOLLY:

I'm not in a hurry.

SAM:

(*Picks up and plays with the hoop*)
I'm sorry, Solly. But that bastard Ernie just upsets
me. He always runs out. He hasn't played that rotten horn for five years now. And him coming on
like he was the great artist of something or other.
Bullshitter.

(*Jaybird again starts to Leach but stops and sits.*)

SOLLY:

How is he?

COWBOY:

Not good.

SOLLY:

Shall I get a doctor?

COWBOY:

No, not yet. No use of all of us getting in trouble.

SAM:

I remember when that bastard Ernie threw a kid
who took an overdose out the window. Didn't even
know whether he was dead or not.

SOLLY:

We never found out for sure.

SAM:

I always believed it.
(*Rolls hoop to the other side of the stage*)

LEACH:

(*Mumbles*)
Three eighty four. Three eighty four. My number's up. I can see it.
(*Laughs crazily*)

JAYBIRD:

Is he dying?
(*Mumbles*)
Why did I start this?
(*Sits next to Solly*)

SOLLY:

I don't blame Ernie for leaving. Listen to that madman.

SAM:

Well, he's alive.

SOLLY:

Which one?
(*Pause*)
I ever tell you the Chinese laundry story? It was in Chicago. I was living above this Chinese laundry and one day the owner knocked on my door and told me that my bathroom was leaking into his store. I told him he could fix it if he wanted to. And he did! Which flipped me because he was a notorious cheap skate. At that time shit was relatively scarce and I had to go out of the city to score. One afternoon I

happened to be sitting on the front fire escape and I noticed some photographers taking pictures of the building. I couldn't figure it out. Besides, I was very high and got paranoid and went inside. That afternoon the headlines were screaming about the biggest narcotics ring in America being rounded up. Where? Downstairs. Two million dollars worth of opium right under my leaking bathroom and I had to go miles to get a pittance. At least I made the front page.

SAM:

That's a good five dollar story.

LEACH:

(*Still in a coma*)
They're coming! Hide! Hide. You can't have me!

SOLLY:

Is he all right?

COWBOY:

The more he talks the better I'll feel.

SOLLY:

Yes, he'll probably live. Whatever that means. I don't think there is such a thing as learning a lesson. At least not with him. Somehow you get the feeling Leach will try again and again until he kills himself. Or the cops get him and he spends a few years in jail. Talking calms me. There is something perverse in me looking for meaning all the time.

LEACH:

Who killed Cock Robin?

(*Insistent*)
Who killed Cock Robin?

COWBOY:

I don't know what he's talking about and I don't know what you're talking about. And once more, babies, I don't care. But, both of you keep blowing. Just blow.

SOLLY:

I can remember that when I was a kid the word marijuana was in the dictionary between marigold and marimba.

SAM:

It probably still is.
(*Lights a book of matches, then stamps them out*)
Hey, man, how long has heroin been illegal?

SOLLY:

In this country since 1928, I think.

SAM:

Why? I mean, man, why did they make it illegal?

SOLLY:

I really don't know. To protect people from themselves. Maybe popular opinion. Maybe the liquor lobby. I once heard it was a plot of the rich. Beats me.

SAM:

I wish I knew.

COWBOY:

Who cares? Man, they got a bomb, haven't they?

Protect us from ourselves. Man, the Japanese cats don't feel that way. That's your theory, Solly. Just a theory. Doesn't have anything to do with us.

SOLLY:

Well, Leach doesn't need any theories, if that's what you mean.

COWBOY:

Everything that's illegal is illegal because it makes more money for more people that way.

SOLLY:

That may be right. But, junk does take its effect.

COWBOY:

We all pay our dues whatever we do.

JAYBIRD:

(*Mumbles incoherently. Wakes up*)
So they all left. What happened to the ending? We've lost the end. Well, well. All's well. Is he dead?

COWBOY:

No.

SOLLY:

You look like the Jaybird I first met.

JAYBIRD:

Mmph. I'm here and you're here. Just like a couple of months ago. Something happened in between. Maybe the idea of an audience. But . . .
(*He touches Solly's shoulder*)

I'm still alone and naïve. And hooked on people.
All sentiment aside, why don't you cats kick junk?

SOLLY:

How many times have we heard someone swearing
he was going to kick?
(*No answer*)
I look out this window and watch the crowds looking into store windows. I try to remember that they
are human beings. Most of the time, it doesn't make
sense. When I talk, I'm a pessimist. Yet, I want to
live. I don't jump into the street against the lights
and just miss killing myself a hundred times a day.
That's what happens out there. And in here, too.
Why are some hunted and others hunt? The tyran-
ny of the majority. I remember once I moved out
of a hotel without paying the old Italian who ran it.
Two months later I was walking by the hotel and
he ran out after me. He wanted to grab me by the
collar and start a fight. Instead he looked at me and
said, "You aren't one of the people." Now what in
God's creation did he mean?
(*Pause on stage.*)

JIM:

(*Enters from audience*)
I'm getting panicked. I'm getting panicked. There's
a rumor the fuzz are coming. The fuzz are coming.
We're going to get busted. Busted. Oh, the pub-
licity! What's wrong with you?

JAYBIRD:

I'm sick. We've lost it. We've lost it.
(*Stands*)

JIM:

What have we lost?

JAYBIRD:

The end, you fool. The end.

JIM:

(*Thinks*)
We'll all die. That's a great idea for you. We just
die.

SOLLY:

Don't be silly. I can't. I'm out of it.

JIM:

That's not the point. How do you propose to get
off stage logically? Ah, you see. Shakespeare, trag-
edy, that sort of thing has been making it for a long
time. This is a time-tested formula. What more can
you ask? I'll die too. Don't think I'm not willing to
die. If it will bring in the revenue. I'll die of exhaus-
tion of carrying you off.
(*Laughs*)
You see? Perfect plot, eh, Jaybird.

JAYBIRD:

You stink!

JIM:

All right so I hired photographers. One of them had
to take a shot.

JAYBIRD:

> I'm not blaming you. How did I ever get into this?
> Oh, yes . . .
> (*Pacing the stage*)
> . . . I wanted to do something far out. Yes, I'm
> guilty of trying to have a little shock value. Is there
> a politician in the house? Then I've failed.

JIM:

> It wasn't your fault. We should have had chicks.
> You planned it with chicks and it was my fault they
> didn't show up. Maybe we'll get them for the movie
> version. Besides I thought you'd be delighted with
> my photographer idea. I thought you liked Dada.

JAYBIRD:

> Shut up!
> (*Long pause*)
> It was my fault. I thought perhaps the doctors
> would take over. That's the message for tonight
> from me. Maybe I'm supposed to be the hero. But
> I'm not a martyr. We don't need women. We need
> a martyr. Let Dada doctors take control of narcotics.

COWBOY:

> Man, doctors wouldn't help me. I'd be out of a job.
> Hell, the doctors would be the big connection.

SOLLY:

> I don't trust them. Those are the people who mildly
> electrocute thousands of people every year. And
> how many prefrontal lobotomies are performed?

Oh, no. I don't trust them as a group any more than I trust the police as a group. Or Junkies, especially the likes of Ernie and Leach.

JAYBIRD:

Yes.

SAM:

Why didn't you get on the H-Bomb riff? If you needed a riff. I've always liked mushrooms.

JIM:

I've had a run for my money.

JAYBIRD:

All right. All right. So that isn't the answer. I've lost it. But one thing I've learned about the theatre. I believe it all fits together.

SOLLY:

It doesn't have to fit.

JAYBIRD:

Yes. Yes, it does. We wouldn't all be on stage if it didn't fit. That's what I had in mind in the first place. I didn't learn anything. I knew it. Find a horror. Then you try to tell people it isn't a horror. And then I have the gall to be horrified. Well, if it wasn't junk, I would have been involved with something else.
(*Takes off Cowboy's red bandana*)

COWBOY:

Well, doctor, that's very heroic.
(*Loud knocking on the door.*)

JAYBIRD:

No doctors, no heroes, no martyrs, no Christs. That's a very good score. I didn't get burned. Maybe short counted, but not burned.

(*Pacing*)

It's all yours now.

(*Pause on stage. Jim opens the door. It is Harry. He performs his record ritual. Lights slowly fade. Music ends in the dark.*)

END